Ibn Battuta
Son of the Mighty Eagle

ABD AL-RAHMAN AZZAM

Illustrated by Khalid Seydo

CASTLEBRIDGE P.S.
LIBRARY

Copyright © Hood Hood Books 1996

Hood Hood Books
29 Bolingbroke Grove
London SW11 6EJ

British Library Cataloguing-in-Publication Data
A catalogue record for this book is available from the British Library

ISBN 1 900251 14 0

No part of this book may be reproduced
in any form without the prior permission of the publishers.
All rights reserved.

Origination by Media Line s.a.l. / ClockWise
Printed by IPH in Egypt

The Story so Far ...

In 1325 Ibn Battuta, a 21 year old scholar and religious judge set off from his hometown in Tangier to perform the pilgrimage to Mecca. First he travelled across the North African desert where he had to keep a watchful eye for bandits and cut-throats, until he reached Egypt. There, he decided to travel south where he came across a Governor who worshipped the sun, and a religious judge whose depth of knowledge was matched only by the size of his turban. Having reached the port of Aydhab where he hoped to cross the Red Sea, he discovered that war made it too dangerous to travel further and he had to retrace his steps until he reached Damascus in Syria. There, he set off with the pilgrims' caravan. On the way, however, the caravan had to cross the dreaded Valley of Doom where, it is said, a fierce wind blows directly from Hell.

Having completed the pilgrimage, Ibn Battuta then travelled to Shiraz and Isfahan where he was shocked by the Mongol destruction and delighted by the delicious apricots. The time however had come for him to return home. Or so he thought ....

CASTLEBRIDGE P.S.
LIBRARY

GLOSSARY

HOURI   A Maiden of Paradise.

JELLABA   A long gown worn by men.

QADI   A religious judge.

QAT   A green leaf chewed by many people in the East to make them relax.

NORTH ATLANTIC OCEAN

EUROPE

TANGIER

SOUTH ATLANTIC OCEAN

AFRICA

CAIRO

DAMASCUS
BAGHDAD

JERUSALEM

MEDINA
MECCA
JEDDAH

ADE

MOGADISHU

MOMBASA

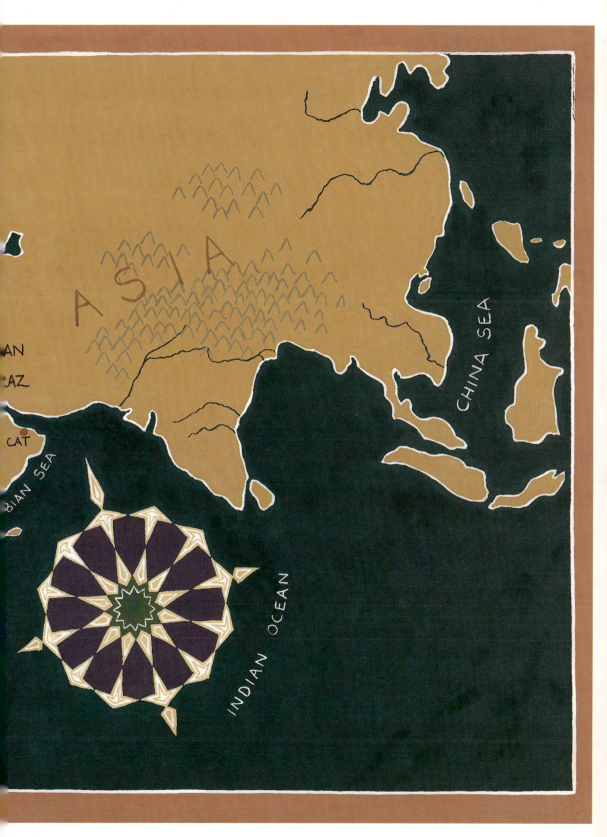

CHAPTER ONE

It was Ibn Battuta's plan to remain in Baghdad for a few weeks, visiting the historical places and meeting the scholarly and holy men of the city. But plans are often made to be discarded. Ibn Battuta did not yet know that he would stay in Baghdad only a few days, and that he would soon find himself on the way to India.

Now, although in those days few people travelled widely, and maps were rather basic, even the doziest of crows could tell you that India was not the quickest way of returning to Tangier. And yet it was to India that Ibn Battuta was heading, and if the most learned historians ever tried to understand why he did so, they would discover that it was because of some mint tea and some love poetry.

Just before his arrival in Baghdad, when the capital city was no more than a day's journey away, Ibn Battuta felt tired and thirsty. Spotting a straw hut in the distance, he decided to halt there. At the entrance of this hut sat an old man in a *jellaba* with so many patches on it that it was difficult to see whether he was wearing a *jellaba* with patches on it - or whether all the patches had somehow come together to make up a new *jellaba*. The old man greeted Ibn Battuta warmly and soon the two men were sitting in the shade of the hut sipping mint tea.

"What a strange place this is," remarked Ibn Battuta, "a hut in the middle of nowhere. What do you do all day ?"

"I recite love poetry," replied the old man, "for you see this may look like a straw hut, but it is much much more than that." Then, seeing Ibn Battuta's puzzled expression, Bilgrami - for that was the old man's name - smiled, "Let me explain... Many years ago, there lived in Baghdad a young prince who fell in love with a noblewoman with whom he should not have fallen in love. He did not wish to fall in love with her, but, you see, the heart has a mind of its own. Marriage was impossible for this young couple, and her father decided that it would be best if he sent his daughter away from Baghdad.

"The young prince was distraught. He could neither eat nor sleep. His hair remained uncombed and his beard unkempt. Slowly he was going mad. Each day he rode out to the outskirts of Baghdad, to this very spot where we are now sitting, hoping for a glimpse of his beloved, and each day he returned home heart-broken.

"The fever of love would not break and the angels who circled above the prince became alarmed. They knew that of all the precious things which God had created in His universe, the most precious was Love. But they also knew that these two young lovers were not destined to be together. It was already written that she would die young, in India, while giving birth to a baby girl who would become one of the world's greatest mathematicians. The young prince however, would live to be 129 years old. He did so much good in his long life that when, finally, he exhaled his last breath, the Caliph himself declared a day of mourning throughout the Empire.

"And yet the fever would not break and, to the alarmed angels, it seemed that the young prince would never reach 129. Each day they accompanied him to this spot, where some would shelter him from the sun, while others would flap their wings to keep him cool. One or two of the younger angels would even glance over to the horizon in the hope of glimpsing the prince's beloved, even though at that very moment she was crossing the

Indus river. Clearly, something had to be done, and something was done, and that, my friend, is why I am here."

The old man paused, took a deep breath and poured Ibn Battuta some more mint tea.

"One night the young prince had a dream in which he saw what had to be done and, upon waking, the fever had magically broken. With half his wealth he bought this piece of land and built upon it a small hut which he turned into a refuge, a refuge for the broken-hearted. To this hut could come anyone who had had their heart broken. Here they would be given some mint tea and a poet would recite verses of love poetry; they could sit quietly, away from the troubles of the world while they waited for their fever to break.

"Now, with the remainder of his money, the young prince ensured that this refuge would carry on long after his death. The years have become decades and 17 poets have resided here before me. I am paid a modest salary, and I go about my work. For you see, my friend, I too am a doctor, but I am a doctor of an illness from which people do not wish to be cured."

With these words, Bilgrami stood up and took a couple of steps away from Ibn Battuta. Then, turning his back, for from experience he knew that poetry often made strong men weep, he began to recite some of the love poetry of his day.

I use the choicest papyri
when I write to you.
I draw my letters
with hammered gold
and lapis lazuli.

Only my name is written with ashes,
for your love has burnt my heart and my name,
for you have consumed all my thought.

When you enter it is day
even at dusk.
When you smile
the orchards open in bloom
even in autumn
When you go
It is desert night
even in spring.

I can call you only by the words
which blossom out of your name,
I can offer you only those gems
which always belonged to you,
but they are covered, my friend
with the ashes of my lost name.

For the next hour Bilgrami's poetry transported Ibn Battuta on a magic carpet of love to a land ruled over by the King of Harmony and the Queen of Beauty who decreed that only tears of joy were ever shed. It was a land where princes and princesses exchanged brief kisses under moonlit, starry skies, and where the lover and the beloved magically became One. Truly, Ibn Battuta reflected, Love was God's greatest creation.

Silence followed the poetry, and then, much to Ibn Battuta's surprise, a deep sigh came from the depths of the hut. He jumped up, astonished to discover that they were not alone. From the shade of the hut emerged a man whose face was young but whose eyes were old. He was dressed in the finest clothes and spoke with such elegance and refinement that Ibn Battuta was convinced that he was someone who yielded great power and influence.

" I apologise for startling you," the man said, his lips breaking into a faint smile, "I did not intend to, but I cannot control my soul."

"Very few men can," replied Ibn Battuta, smiling. The man appeared to soften and he now approached with his hand outstretched,

"Let me introduce myself. My name is Nizam al-Mulk. I am named after my ancestor the great Vizier. I, too, am a Vizier. Indeed, every member of my family is a Vizier. I think it runs in the blood."

"And I am Ibn Battuta from Tangier. My ancestor was a duck, and scholarship runs in my blood!"

Nizam al-Mulk laughed out loud. "It is a great pleasure to meet you, but are you not a long way from home?"

"Thanks to Bilgrami's poetry, I was, only a few moments ago, back in my mother's arms. And for whom do you sigh?"

Now there were no longer any smiles or laughter. Nizam al-Mulk's face appeared much older, almost as if twenty years had passed in a brief second. "For my beautiful wife and baby daughter whom the plague carried away," he answered.

"Straight to Paradise, I am certain," replied Ibn Battuta.

"Will you ride with me to Baghdad?" asked the Vizier.

"Gladly," replied Ibn Battuta.

As the two men mounted their horses, Ibn Battuta noticed how the Vizier tried to slip a bag of coins into Bilgrami's hand. The old man pushed it away, and then, smiling softly, he whispered, "You can reward me, Sire, when you are well and your fever has broken."

CHAPTER TWO

On their journey to Baghdad, Nizam al-Mulk told Ibn Battuta that he was the Vizier of the Mongol Emperor who was currently passing on his way to Tabriz.

"The Mongol Emperor, himself!" exclaimed Ibn Battuta in admiration.

"Himself."

"The Mongol Emperor? The descendant of the fierce Chengiz Khan and the brutal Hulagu?"

Nizam al-Mulk smiled enigmatically, "That is correct."

Ibn Battuta's thoughts ran wild with images of fierce, snarling, brutal, gnarling Mongols who had once sacked Baghdad and killed the Caliph, and then sacked every other city and killed everyone else.

"Would you like to meet him?" Nizam al-Mulk's words recalled Ibn Battuta from his thoughts.

"Meet him?" he piped, "is it safe?"

"Let me tell you about the Emperor. He is not quite as ferocious as Chengiz Khan or Hulagu. But if you do meet him, you must remember three things. Firstly, the Emperor thinks himself a philosopher."

"A philosopher?" Ibn Battuta was astounded, "the Emperor of the Mongols is a philosopher?"

"A philosopher."

"Is he a good philosopher?"

"The first time I met him," Nizam al-Mulk related, "the Emperor asked why it was that if a man reads many books and gains much knowledge, his head does not weigh more."

"And how did you answer?"

"I replied that only he who possesses an astute enough brain could answer such a complex and subtle question."

Ibn Battuta laughed aloud, "I can see that diplomacy runs through your blood! But tell me, what school of philosophy does the Emperor follow?"

"Oh that is easy to answer," replied Nizam al-Mulk, "He follows the 'I am the Emperor of the Mongols who are the fiercest people alive and who do not simply enjoy, but actually relish chopping off people's heads, but please feel free to disagree with me' school. I am sure that you have heard of it."

"Of course," laughed Ibn Battuta, "I studied it diligently as a student in Tangier! So what is the second thing I should know about the Emperor?"

"Well, he is not only a philosopher but also a poet."

"A philosopher and a poet! I assume that he is an excellent poet?" remarked Ibn Battuta.

"The Mongol school of poetry resembles the Mongol school of philosophy very, very closely."

"But seriously," remarked Ibn Battuta, "why do you stay with him?"

"When a ruler has great power, he can do great evil, but he can also do good. Now that I have lost my wife and my daughter, now that the sun never rises but only sets for me, my life is devoted to reducing the evil and increasing the good."

"It is a very noble cause."

"On the contrary, it is a very selfish one. For you see, my wife and daughter are in Paradise and I am desperate to join them there. So I spend my life doing good."

For a while the two men rode in silence, then Ibn Battuta asked,

"By the way, what is the third thing I should know about the Emperor?"

"He lisps very badly," replied Nizam al-Mulk, "but since he is the Emperor of the Mongols, he does not. Do you understand?"

"I underthtand," replied Ibn Battuta.

For the second time that day, Nizam al-Mulk smiled, "You would make a fine diplomat."

"NEVER!" shrieked the Mongol Emperor, "NEVER!"

It was the following day and, true to his word, Nizam al-Mulk was in the process of introducing Ibn Battuta to the Emperor, only for him to leap up from the dais upon which he was sitting, his face red with outrage, shrilling, "NEVER!"

Never what? a petrified Ibn Battuta thought. Never would I return to Tangier? Never would my head rest again on my shoulders? And for a brief moment he thought of all the beautiful turbans he had bought.

In the meantime, the Emperor was continuing to shriek, "Thith man cannot be the Thon of a Thmall Duck. Never! From now on he will be called the Thon of The Mighty Eagle."

Ibn Battuta, eyes lowered, was speechless, but the Emperor certainly was not. "Yeth! Thon of the Mighty Eagle. Much better. Much, much better. In fact I feel inthpired, I feel a poem coming on."

At once his whole court fell silent. No one dared speak, move, or even breathe. Slowly and pompously (except of course the Emperor could not possibly be pompous) the Emperor stood up and, in what he thought was a moving and artistic tone, he recited his poem.

The Thmall Duck quacketh
But the Mighty Eagle doth not!

Exhausted, he now fell back. "Oh what it is to be a poet! It is thuch a burden. How heavy my heart feelth. Now, leave me," he ordered, "I am tired and a poet needth hith retht."

Thus ended Ibn Battuta's only audience with the Mongol Emperor. He had expected to meet the descendant of Chengiz Khan, but instead had met someone who was probably the descendant of the great Khan's hairdresser. Still, he thought, it was a relief not to have lost his head.

CHAPTER THREE

IBN BATTUTA REMAINED IN BAGHDAD for a few days. Time had been cruel to the city; power and wealth had led to corruption, and the Mongols had brought devastation. As he walked its streets, he could almost hear the glorious and triumphant processions echoing from its walls. Almost! For Ibn Battuta had seen enough on his travels to understand that once the wheel of fortune turns, mighty civilisations are reduced, in the blink of an eye, to handfuls of dust.

Ibn Battuta, however, was a troubled young man. Ever since his meeting with Bilgrami, he could not get the story of the young prince out of his mind. Could love really drive a man to despair? Bilgrami had told him that the young woman had died giving birth to a girl by the name of Gulruh - Spirit of the Rose - who was a great mathematician. She would, he imagined, be an old lady by now. And yet, did she know about the hut - built in memory of her mother - where love never died?

It was then that Ibn Battuta decided to travel to India to find Gulruh. India, he imagined, was not much larger than Tangier, so how difficult could it be to find a mathematician who went by the name of Spirit of the Rose?

To reach India in those days, Ibn Battuta had to retrace his steps back to Mecca, and then to the port of Jeddah. From there he would travel to Aden or Muscat and then to India. However, in order to do so, Ibn Battuta had, for the first time in his life, to set foot on a boat. To date, although he had travelled widely, he had never left land. As a young boy in Tangier, he had seen hundreds of boats sail in and out of the city's port, but had never been courageous enough to board one. This meant that even now, despite his title of Qadi, he still half-believed that on the open seas huge one-eyed sea monsters patiently waited for ships. The monsters would drag them down to the ocean's bottom where sunken treasures and lost cities awaited the doomed travellers.

However, not even in the wildest imagination of a court poet could the tiny, squeaky, shabby, creaky boats, ranged next to each other in the port of Jeddah, be compared to the sleek sailing vessels he had seen in Tangier. To him, it appeared impossible that these boats could set sail without at once sinking. Half their planks had been rotted and eroded by the sea, and were held together by nothing more than the threads of coconut fibre and optimisim.

A desolate Ibn Battuta stood quietly, staring with disbelief upon the creaking vessels, when he noticed, standing next to him, a smiling Yemeni. Clearly, he was a pilot of one of the vessels.

"Planning on a trip?" he enquired, somehow managing to speak and smile at the same time.

"Well, I was hoping to travel down to Aden," replied Ibn Battuta, "but all the vessels are full."

By now, the Yemeni was grinning like a cat at a fishmongers. "Aden? but that is only a stone's throw from here! I am a humble pilot, son of a humble pilot, son of a humble pilot, son of Ismail, Aden's first and only blind barber. If you will do me the honour, let me be your humble servant and take you to Aden."

Ibn Battuta felt humbled, "You mean, you have space on your boat?"

"Space!" The Yemeni, who went by the name of Ali, was almost jumping up and down with excitment, "Space! I can assure you, honoured traveller, you will be the only passenger!"

For a brief moment, a moment upon which he would later rufuly reflect upon, Ibn Battuta was suspicious. He was almost tempted to ask why, with all the vessels full, was Ali's vessel empty. But by this stage, Ali was in such a state of ecstasy, that he did not have the heart to ask any inconvenient questions.

"Where is your vessel?" he enquired.

"My vessel, O honourable sir! O learned Judge! my vessel is only a few minutes away."

"And when can we sail?"

"Whenever it pleases your Eminence!"

"You assure me," asked Ibn Battuta, "that I will be the only passenger?"

"O definitely so, O sagest of sages!"

"Then," exclaimed Ibn Battuta, infected by Ali's optimism, "let us sail!"

The trouble with optimism, as a wise philosopher once wrote, is that it can let you down. Ali was true to his word; there were no other human passengers on board. What he had failed to say, however, was that the vessel was carrying, laden, creaking with, full of, camels. All sorts of camels: she camels and he camels, old camels and young camels and every single camel, every single one, was smiling.

By then, it was too late for Ibn Battuta to turn back. He had given his word to Ali, and so he set sail, for the first time, in a poor man's ark with a smiling Yemeni and countless smiling camels. Quickly, too quickly for Ibn Battuta's liking, the land disappeared from view and the vessel cut its way through the choppy waters of the Red Sea.

"It is a great honour to have a fellow-passenger," exclaimed Ali, by now almost laughing out loud. "Not to say that I have anything against my friends here. Camels are very, very wise. Often I have deep philosophical discussions with them. They have some extremely interesting views, you know."

Ibn Battuta remained silent, counting the minutes until he could see land again. He was stuck in the middle of the Red Sea with a demented sailor who held philosophical discussions with camels. At the same time, whenever the vessel hit a wave, he felt his stomach in his mouth. Things, he reflected, could not get any worse.

They did. Out of the corner of his eye, Ibn Battuta noticed some movement. On turning round, to his horror, he saw a shark's fin protruding from the waters. They, Ibn Battuta, Ali, and his horde of smiling camels, were not alone. A hungry shark, patiently awaiting his lunch, was tailing them!

Ibn Battuta was seized with terror. Though he tried to speak, no words came out. All he could do was nudge Ali and point to the shark.

"O yes, a shark," Ali remarked with no care in the world. "Poor shark! He seems so hungry. Poor, poor shark!"

Ibn Battuta was dumbfounded. So that, he despaired, was how it was all going to end! In the midst of a hungry shark, a smiling sailor and some philosophical camels. At the same time, the sea refused to be still, and Ibn Battuta felt as if his stomach wanted to re-acquaint itself with every meal it had ever eaten. His mind now raced: camels, sharks, apricots, love poetry, turbans, camels wearing turbans, the waves, more waves, up and down, up and down, philosophical sharks .... it was all too much, and Ibn Battuta, the intrepid land traveller, fainted onto the deck of Ali's vessel.

Do people dream when they faint? Perhaps not, but when one has chosen to sail in the midst of camels and is being chased by a hungry shark, does life then not resemble a dream? A wise Chinese sage once enquired whether, when a man dreams that he is a butterfly, is he a man dreaming that he is a butterfly, or is he a butterfly dreaming that he is a man? Did Ibn Battuta dream that he was a camel, or was he a camel dreaming that he was Ibn

Battuta? No matter, now he was resting in Paradise and his fevered brow was being cooled by a piece of heavenly silk, dipped in the cool waters of the rivers of Eden.

Ibn Battuta's time on earth, however, had not yet come to an end, and he was destined to live for many more years. It would have been extremely unfortunate had he died on the vessel, for at that precise moment his guardian-angel was absent. For you see, in those days people did not travel far, and the angel sent from Heaven to accompany Ibn Battuta on this earth, thought that he would have an easy life in Tangier. Little did he know - for angels are there only to obey orders - that he would spend his time chasing after this young Moroccan who simply refused to remain in one place! So it happened that when the angel saw Ibn Battuta board the vessel from Jeddah, he decided that he would take a rest and then catch up with him in Aden. It was lucky for him that Ibn Battuta did arrive safely, or else the angel would have had to do some serious explaining to the senior angel.

In the meantime, Ibn Battuta was busy having his forehead cooled by a *houri* from Paradise, or at least he was dreaming that he was. Even if the reality was slightly different - he was in fact having his face licked by one of Ali's more affectionate camels - it mattered little, for, on opening his eyes, he saw, ahead of him, the port of Aden. The sea was now calm and the shark, probably disgusted by Ibn Battuta's weakness, had swum away.

Ibn Battuta rose shakily to his feet.

"Ah! had a good sleep?" asked Ali.

Ibn Battuta smiled weakly. "I see that we have reached our destination. How much do I owe you?"

Ali, however, refused to accept any money, "It was a great honour to have transported such a learned man. How can I possibly accept any money?"

"I suppose you were coming to Aden anyway to sell the camels?"

Ali looked aghast, "Sell my camels? Sell my dearest friends, my travelling companions, my soul-mates?" His eyes began to water, "Would you sell members of your own family? Would you sell your friends? Sell my camels! Are you mad?"

Some questions are not meant to be answered, and Ibn Battuta remained discreetly silent. Nevertheless, Ali had kindly brought him to Aden and he simply had to find a way to repay him. Perhaps a gift? Ibn Battuta thought and thought, when suddenly in a moment of Heaven-sent inspiration, everything became clear. *QAT!!* that was it! He had read how the Yemenis often chewed this leaf which made them relaxed. Well, Ibn Battuta smiled to himself, Ali must have chewed enough *qat* to take him to the Day of Judgement and slightly beyond.

"If you do not accept any money as payment, maybe you would allow me to buy you a small gift.... perhaps some *qat*?"

In a flash Ali was out of the vessel, and Ibn Battuta found himself being dragged by his sleeve through Aden's bustling market, until the two men were standing in front of a shop where *qat* leaves were protruding from every corner. The shop owner greeted Ali as if he were a long-lost brother. Indeed, Ibn Battuta noted, he greeted every passer-by in the same manner.

"Ali! my dearest Ali. How are you? and how are Barquq, Zarquq and Marquq?"

Ali glanced over to Ibn Battuta and whispered proudly, "My camels!"

"They are fine", he replied, "and they send their warmest greetings. But enough talk, let me introduce you to my dearest friend, Ibn Wizwooza (Son of the Small Goose). He has come all the way from Jeddah to try your *qat* leaves."

"In fact ..." Ibn Battuta tried to interject, but it was too late for the shop owner had heard Ali's magic words, "and he has money to spend". Before another word could be uttered, the three men were sitting inside the shop, cups of steaming tea in their hands and a ball of *qat* leaves in each of their mouths.

"So, tell me," the shop owner, who went by the name of Yusuf, asked Ibn Battuta, "why are you called Son of the Small Goose?"

"Actually, I am not," replied Ibn Battuta, "my name means Son of the Small Duck."

"Ah!" Ali and Yusuf both nodded their heads sagely, as if everything was now clear.

And in fact, remarkably enough, it was. The more Ibn Battuta chewed on his leaves, the easier life became, so that after an hour (or was it a day?) the three men had put the world to right. After a couple of hours, they had agreed that Ibn Battuta would travel no more and would remain in Aden, where he would open a *qat* shop and would marry one of Yusuf's fourteen (or was it forty-one?) sisters. After three hours (or was it seventeen years?) the three men were fast asleep; and such is the sweet and forgiving nature of *qat*, that upon waking, all the promises made had been instantly forgotten.

Ibn Battuta woke up before the two men and, groggily getting to his feet, gathered his belongings and stepped out of the shop into the bright sunlight of Aden.

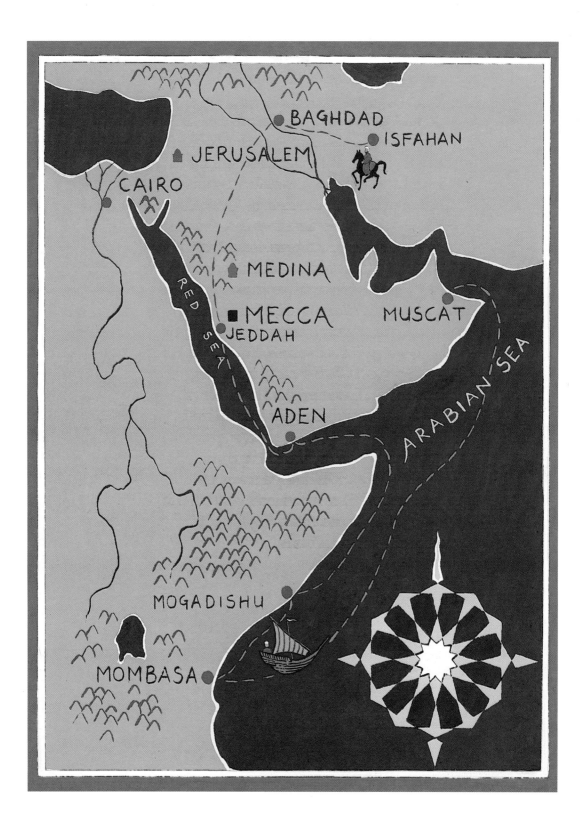

CHAPTER FOUR

The port of ADEN WAS VISITED by merchants from India, Ceylon and China. It was also an exceedingly hot place and the monsoon was at its peak. This meant that, until the winds died down, no direct voyages to India could be made. The city itself was brimming full with almost all imaginable goods: spices, herbs, cottons, pearls and beads, brass and bronze, Indian silks and Chinese porcelain, African ivory and tropical fruits. The city's merchants were exceedingly wealthy, and as Ibn Battuta discovered one day, extremely competitive as well.

While strolling through the port's opulent market, Ibn Battuta came across a melee of people all surrounding a ram. There was much shouting and yelling and the people were becoming very agitated. Clearly, none had recently chewed any *qat*! Ibn Battuta was told that there was only one ram for sale that day, and there were many merchants who wished to buy it. Soon, the merchants were bidding against each other until finally the ram was sold for the astronomical sum of 400 dinars!

With the Indian ports closed, Ibn Battuta decided to risk another sea voyage and joined a vessel which was sailing down the coast of Africa. It was an opportunity to visit a few cities he had read about until the monsoon calmed down. Departing from Aden, the ship sailed for four days until it reached the city of Zaila which he found to be the dirtiest, most disagreeable and most stinking city in the world. The reason for this was that fresh fish and camels were slaughtered daily in its streets, causing a stench so unpleasant, that Ibn Battuta quickly beat a retreat to the vessel.

A few days later, Ibn Battuta arrived in Mogadishu, where, as a Qadi, he was warmly welcomed. He was escorted to the Governor's residence where he washed and then was dressed in the finest linen and silk. A feast was then prepared for him. Dish after dish of the most delicious food was placed in front of him: meat, chicken, fish, vegetables, bananas in milk, pickled lemons, and above all, a mystery fruit which made him forget the apricots of Shiraz. It was green on the outside and orange on the inside, its texture was smooth and its aroma heavenly. It was deliciously sweet when ripe, but could also be eaten unripe when it tasted like a lemon. It was, decided Ibn Battuta, the perfect fruit and, on asking its name, was told that it was called a mango.

From Mogadishu, Ibn Battuta travelled to Mombassa and Zanzibar, until he reached Kilwa, the city of gold. The gold trade which centred around Kilwa made the city and its inhabitants extremely wealthy. Ibn Battuta noted how people lived in three-storey stone houses which had indoor plumbing. They wore cotton and silk garments and ate from plates of Chinese porcelain.

In Kilwa, Ibn Battuta came across another fruit, the like of which he had never seen before. He was told that it reddens the face and fattens the body when eaten. When ripe it is green and, if one cuts out a piece of its rind with a knife and makes a hole in the head of the nut, one can drink a liquid of extreme sweetness from it. Once the liquid has been drunk, the pulp is then spooned out and eaten. Both milk and honey are made from its oil. Ibn Battuta was intrigued and asked its name. He was told that it came from India and was called a coconut.

For the past three months, Ibn Battuta had been meandering down the African coast, but with summer approaching, he had

to sail back if he ever hoped to reach India. And so, Ibn Battuta boarded a vessel and, three weeks later, found himself in the Gulf of Oman.

Cut off from the rest of Arabia by the sea on three sides and the desert on the fourth, the city of Muscat looked towards India for its living. Indian traders sold luxuries there which were bound for Arabia and Europe. Having endured some of the hottest regions on earth, during which time he had crossed the equator, Ibn Battuta rested for a few weeks before finding a vessel which would take him to India - except that no vessels were going to India. The moonsoon winds had closed all the ports and, for the next few months, no voyage was possible.

It was at this stage that Ibn Battuta made a decision that has left historians scratching their heads in bewilderment. He decided that if he could not sail directly to India, he would instead retrace his steps to Mecca, travel to Cairo, to Syria and then, heading north, through Turkey, he would reach India. To him the idea seemed simple, really quite obvious, and meant that he could avoid any sea voyages.

As he was making preparations to cross the desert to Mecca, he thought he could hear a deep sigh. However, since he was quite alone, it could only have been the wind blowing. If only he had looked above him, he might just have noticed a haggard-looking guardian-angel wondering when this young Moroccan was ever going to return home.

The Travels of Ibn Battuta
Ibn Battuta in th Valley of Doom
Ibn Battuta Son of the Mighty Eagle

CASTLEBRIDGE P.S.
LIBRARY